Heartspan

Heartspan

Poems, Humorous to Sarcastic to Serious

David Davis

BOOKLOGIX®
Alpharetta, Georgia

Copyright © 2023 by David Davis

All rights reserved. No part of this book may be reproduced or transmitted in any form or by any means, electronic or mechanical, including photocopying, recording, or any information storage and retrieval system, without permission in writing from the author.

ISBN: 978-1-6653-0715-4 - Paperback
ISBN: 978-1-6653-0716-1 - Hardcover
eISBN: 978-1-6653-0717-8 - eBook

These ISBNs are the property of BookLogix for the express purpose of sales and distribution of this title. The content of this book is the property of the copyright holder only. BookLogix does not hold any ownership of the content of this book and is not liable in any way for the materials contained within. The views and opinions expressed in this book are the property of the Author/Copyright holder, and do not necessarily reflect those of BookLogix.

Library of Congress Control Number: 2023916861

Printed in the United States of America

☉This paper meets the requirements of ANSI/NISO Z39.48-1992 (Permanence of Paper)

0 9 1 1 2 3

These are for Kathy and Elizabeth, who had to live through a good part of it and deserve as much credit as they can get.

Introduction

I don't know if these are my best poems, or even if they are good poems. But they are the ones I like. They are in roughly chronological order from when I was very young to now when I am very old.

The World's a Stage

The world's a stage
The setting and the props are fake
All the people are actors quoting lines somebody else wrote
The author's crazy, the director's drunk, and the producer's on vacation
In other words, things are all mixed up
The heroine forgot her part
The hero can't find the door
And if the stage doesn't collapse
I think the audience is going to start throwing tomatoes
And if I weren't so busy laughing
I think I would cry.

A Girl's Smile

A girl's smile is a masterpiece
Could I have created yours?
Can I take some little credit
For once having made you
Laugh, made you smile
Made you happy for an instant?
If I have made you smile
I have created a masterpiece
Could any man want more?

My Heart Died

My dear, my heart died a long time ago
I miss it now and then
When I see a person cry
    because he is happy
Or when I see beauty
    a girl, a flower, a poem on a wall
I know the emotion, the feeling
But, like I said, my heart died
    a long time ago
And I miss it now and then.

To a Girl Who Should be Sitting on a Library Wall Overlooking San Antonio

Black upon black
Form upon form
She sits
Gently
On the stone wall
The night-lit city
A beautiful painting
Destined to fall pale
As her backdrop
Dark pervades
Except for the white city lights
And her white, eye-lit face
My childhood returns
And finds form
In her face
It becomes, somehow
A thing I can understand
And therein lies the beauty
I find
In that silhouette of white.

About a Not Too Good Statue of Christ Nailed to the Wall of a Church

That's a heck of a thing to do to a Christ
To wrap him up in rags, give him a bloated belly like a corpse
And hang him from a wall or something
He's even got his head down
Like he lost

That isn't my God, brother
Mine is tough and hard
Used to walking all day
And fighting if the need arose
My God looks you straight in the eye
And hasn't lost a fight yet
      And I'm betting he isn't going to
And the last thing you would be able to do
      Is hang him up on anything
         For more than a few days

That isn't my God, Mac
My God doesn't just hang around
He climbs down and starts the revolution.

The Game

She stood by the rail overlooking the basketball court
The teams were warming up, and the long, high-arched shots
    flew by her face
I, a crowd-hidden figure in the bleachers, stared past the team
    up at her
She looked rather lonely and forlorn just standing there
    above the end of the court
She stayed all through the first half, and whenever the play
    swung to her end of the court, I watched her,
    not the ball
She left at halftime, my attention returned to the game
    and we lost.

Epitaph for a Mass Slave Grave Written by a Southern White over One Hundred Years Later

Here they lie, Black slaves, now free
Gone where there ain't no segregation
Now they know the truth I learned in youth
That God's a big brown Jew-boy
Praise the Lord and pass the cornbread

Amen, Brother.

Lights That Wink in the Night

Lights that wink in the night
The church on the hill, steeple aglow
Teiane's bar by the road, windows curtained
The My-T-Fine Bar-B-Que, low-lit and empty
The gas station, closed forever
The first bright, then dim lights from the coming cars
High, low, bright, dim
Come on, buddy, dim 'em
And forever the reflectors by the side of the road
That glow only when someone shines their lights on them

I knew a reflector once
Not a bad guy to have around
More dependable than a lamp
But not quite as romantic
Come to think of it, I knew a church once
But she never got out enough
I expect she would have been an old maid
Except an old radical married her
Not much sense, these radicals
I guess he thought he could change her
The bar I knew, she's in LA now
We never really made it
We just didn't fit
I ran one way, she ran another
The bar-b-que is an OK guy
Good to sit around with and talk to
But bar-b-que is going out of style
Only a few left, mostly in the South
Most folks just don't have time for bar-b-que anymore
The gas station is closed too
Just like the one by the road
The new ones, no pop, no candy, no pot-bellied stoves

My kids will never know that old man
And I don't think I could ever explain a pot-bellied stove anyway
The reflector is in the army now
Like I said, a nice guy to have around
But not the kind you invite into the kitchen

As each headlight passes, they seem to grow brighter
Blurring my vision
It makes my eyes water
I know I'm on the right road
To get where I'm going
But I wish that sometime
I could come back by
And stop at the church to pray
Get a little bar-b-que, a little gas
And warm myself by that old stove
And follow the reflectors home
But even as I pass
I know they are gone.

A Girl

A canyon behind a blouse
A waterfall over a neck
A guitar walks
      on the most important part of a miniskirt.

Mana

Canary, my free bird
Your spirit lifts o're your song
Soaring skyward
Making reason dance the Virginia Reel
Every free thing must love you
For you are most free
For all of us poets
God in his mercy
Made thee.

Over an Antarctic of Clouds

Over an Antarctic of clouds
I flew through sunset's rainbow
From blue to red to darkness

From home to home via Atlanta
The flyboys' way to go.

The Birthday Present

A music stand that folds and tucks away
But pops back out when I want to play
A surprise, I admit, as love always is
You'd think I would learn after twenty years
A dollar here, a dollar there
Dollars I know they could not spare
So is love expressed
Even on a day when it is legal
To say I love you.

Screenplay for an Affair of the Mind

fade in	p	a girl
	a	
haze	s	a glimpse
	s	
focus		class together
	t	
sound	w	hello
	o	
beauty		silent I love you
	y	
diffraction lens	e	no response
	a	
distort	r	another man
	s	
slow fade		she moves on

To Lenelle, Who Let Me Sing with Her

I realize
as do those who hear me
that I shall have to die
and go to heaven
before my voice
becomes angelic
As a certain voice instructor
so aptly put it
I have
the Voice of a Peanut

But even if heaven
should bring me
harmony
it could not purchase
the pleasure
of singing
here
now
at your side

Of things in this world
I love
singing
is one of the few
It is the joy
of a hidden soul
communicating

You allowed me this joy
Your spirit is more beautiful
than your voice.

Song, a Prose Poem

Moon dark light shine on hazel hair rose. Star shine light shine song shine on this love of mine. Sing song to tune play my guitar. I call you call wonder where you are?

Rosebud red rambling on soul feet of clay. Can I call you call on night or day. Rosebud red romance shall call it someday. I sing if you sing we sing on a day. Love with proper connotations, sing your own song. Such sights as a true love sing their own song. Sing song dark moonshine, sing song of today. Sing song to my tune, in harmony me. Call woman ramble, I'm gone someday. My songs have endings, come what may. If you sing with my song know soon I'll be gone.

So sang the young man to his love on a day. He taught her his song and was soon gone away. Now sings she a ramble, and rambles a day by the dark of the moonshine and the light of the song. Sing song red ramble, I'll sing you a lay to keep you from moonshine and the cold of the day. Are you hazel hair rose all gone away? Sing not by the moonshine, for he's all gone away.

Her Breast Lay Lightly

Her breast lay lightly in the curve of the guitar
Her voice gently on my ear
We sang unafraid
As sparking fingers danced on strings
We courted in melody
Loved in rhythm
And grew in time
Life is not a song
The song is life.

Three Relative Quanta

c plus c equals c
1 plus 1 equals 1
Bother me not with reason old man
The universe has its own logic

Lambda equals h over p sheds light upon light
Uniting contradiction
Its existence forcing the world
To change its mind

Delta p delta x equals h bar over 2 means I am not sure
Where I am, or how fast I am going where
But I think maybe I can guess
How far off course I am.

Spring-Sun

The lilacs are a-blooming
Filling the air with grape Kool-Aid
And for those of us
Who live on the border of life
Where flowers are not
       pretty, sweet-smelling things
But miracles
It is time to sing
Our soft, sad tune of blue joy.

Beethoven's Child

(To a Musician Going Deaf)

Such silence you must hear
        amidst your Bach
Such silence, such silence
        feeling your cello's strings
Haunted, haunted by soundless harp

Does Beethoven's madness
        frighten your scarred ears
Such silence, such silence
        behind every note
            every song
            every sound
        of night or man

What melody, what tune, what sound
        would you play
        would you hear
If it were the last
        before again
        such silence.

My Name Is the Beloved

My name is the Beloved
I was born in the land
      of the three Tygers
I grew amid the swamps
       by the great ocean
       in the soft pines
       near the wide river
My ancestors
       from the cool mountains
       from the hot plains
Grew cotton, tobacco, and corn
       preached, taught, and farmed
The land is in their blood
They are where they have been since they came
Family after family
Generation after generation
They are here
And I am here

I wish I was in Texas.

Or So I'm Told

Used to be
(or so I am told)
Women's bodies were expensive
Purchasable only at the price of
        candles by dinner light
        false words
        gold rings
(I'm not sure about all this)
        relatives
        and responsibilities

But along with the body you got
        cooking
        cleaning
        mothering
(I'm not sure I believe all this either)
        supporting
        and loving (Remember that word)

Now
(or so I understand)
Female bodies are
Two for a nickel
Three cents if you only want one
But most, like toasters
        last only a year or two
        (if not dropped)
        and come without
        the extra frills.

Creativity Flows

Creativity flows like concrete too long in the sun
Thoughts ripple like waves in a mosquito pool
I run with the throngs in Death Valley sands
Life blossoms like a lily in December
I forge after dreams like sound chasing light
And am welcomed like a king to a new-found, still empty land.

I Have a Picture

I have a picture of her face
A tape of her sounding voice
But of her scent when she lay
      near me naked
Of her cherry earlobe taste
      tucked between my lips
Of her touch and scratching
      of my palm
I have nothing, only memories

Technology, you have failed me.

The Chrysanthemums Bloomed

The chrysanthemums bloomed
the day I was born
twenty-four years ago
my mother said
she remembers, she says
I don't, but I suppose
if one has to be born
a good day to do it
is the day
the chrysanthemums bloomed.

'Tis Not Heaven

'Tis not heaven I hold here
But my hand
That dances fire
And spins
A universe away.

Feel the Night

Feel the night
Lie with me
We'll find a shadow in the dark
Hide from the stark quarter moon
In a grass hollow below
      the shadow sound
      the fleeing photon
Feel me
Lie with the night
We'll find a silence in the dark
Hide from the mind of our eye
In a caressing touch below
      the shadow thought
      the fleeing mind.

My Night

My night is but a star's wink
So, at times, I take a shorter view
Take the effect of wind
        upon a mountain
Some say the wind wears
        The mountain down
I know better
It is the wind that bends.

Suddenly Old

My father made out his will today
He told me he felt it was time
So why is it I
Who feels suddenly old?

Patriotism

There is a little black girl
        in my yard
Singing the Battle Hymn
        of the Republic
As she rides her tricycle
        up and down the walk
I don't know why
        she sings it now
But it is certainly nice to know
        That patriotism is not dead.

Silent Nights

Silent nights
Crying in the streets
The lights blurred
    in the winked-back tears
Scribbling verses
    on notepads
Dripping emotions
    on pavement
Crying in the shock
    of not being hated
Of not being turned away
    of maybe
Just maybe
    being loved.

The Music of My Soul

They broke the music of my soul
Left my life a pentameter of four measures
An irregular iambic of pointless counterpoint
A sonnet with thirteen rhymes
I cannot sing a song without time
Nor march to a beatless drum
But what use is a sprightly tune
In a city of monotone souls.

A Woman's Room

I had forgotten the scent of a
        woman's room
Having lived too long in my own
        company
Had forgotten that colors
        so cacophonous about me
Could be blended
        into melody
I had forgotten that furniture
        could float
Not stone stand like my
        solid chests
That rooms, like women, could put beauty
        to use.

I Left Her

I left her in a drugstore
In Yuma, Arizona
Waiting for her ship to come in
Which, being in the middle of a desert
Is a strange place to wait for a ship
Unless California drops off
But never mind that
I found out she had disappeared
      later
Searching for a sea
      I guess
Meanwhile, I sit surrounded
      by plaster-white walls
Uncolored by posters or prints
Untouched by nail or tape
Facing myself
Wondering if she will sail by
And tack something up.

This Is No

This is no moon for howling
'Tis but three quarter done
But the song on my heart is a-laden
And I feel my season has come

This is no rock on a mountain
'Tis but a lake by a stone
But the yearn in my heart is a-yowling
And I feel my life starting to moan

Brother wolf, under sky, cunning and sly
Dark of night, he and I, crying so high
Home is to moonward
It must be so
For so we prowl
Down here below

This is no moon for howling
'Tis but three quarters done
But the strains my heart is a-chanting
Are of cold darkly nights like a bone.

Big Things

Big things I understand
It's the little things I don't
Stars are comprehensible to me
Even glimpses of eternity
Truth, justice, are easy to see
People are not so simple
      to be understood by dolts like me
Do flowers understand bees?
Or rivers, seas?
If the space-time curve
      seems in my sight
Or quark's vibrations
      like ABCs
Why is a smile
      such a puzzle?
If an osculating curve
      I can calculate
And Schrödinger's Equation
      derive
Why is a wink
      such a mystery
With a TI 9000 Programmable
And a CRC Handbook besides
Why is the curve of a thigh
      still so damnable?

To Write Again

How good it is to write verse again
Or at least what I, in my non-English major's
      loose way with a term, call verse
To cut a tear on a scrap of tree
      leave a line across tomorrow's mind
      edge a smile of graphite lead
It salves a scrape or two
      chinks an empty crack
      cools a rough and bleeding sore.

Winter

The winter burned brown trees
        stare back at me
Barren and empty
Dormant now, waiting out
        another winter
They know, in these iced months
        of frozen life
That this too will pass
My soul is not so sure.

Not a Sonnet

I cannot, though I try, a sonnet write
It galls my bones a bit when poets meet
And cry aloud their lines of verse so tight
I often sink my head and seek the street
My pen I've tried to fit in many forms
But will not stay contained within the rule
So seems I fail if judged by any norms
And my wild muse a lass that will not school
But when my lines their own awry form find
And thought define the nature of my verse
Let no scholar of rigid eye or mind
Call me to task or leave for me a curse
If I to end my lines a curvéd smile
Or rounded tear or twisted pun compile.

Dissidents

Every now and then
a brave man
stands
and quotes Thoreau
Ah Mother Russia
with your Siberian cold heart
why do they love you
why have so many
given so much
and gotten so little
in return
Why are your lovers
to your cold shoulder
exiled
or expelled
to us
who welcome them
with warm arms and tears
knowing they would prefer
your icy bosom.

My Father

who gave me five hundred dollars
he didn't have
today
spent this evening
asking about my PhD
and telling me
how to brush my teeth
yesterday he told me
how to drive a car
tomorrow
he may tell me
how to tie my shoes
he loves me
he knows that I am a grown
                      educated
                      competent man
but
he does not realize
I am no longer
his little boy.

Crescent Moon

Crescent moon
Single star of love
early evening
Sunday before Christmas
Churches hung with poinsettias
    and song
for some kid
born of a knocked-up girl
and a sneaky spirit
dropped into a trough
surrounded by manure
    and oats
so we could chop down trees
sell presents
and get fat
Sing a song of joy.

I Have Witnesses

I have witnesses
They have seen it all
The chill stars
Glinting on the pale dogwoods
And the blue lace lilacs
Of another Spring
They have seen it all
The Fall, and Rise
The Time
My not-yet-thirty summers
See only shadows
Leaf green mists
By streetlamps lit
Hints of what was
And Is
Even in my winter
Long past youth
I will not have seen it all
But I have witnesses
And they have seen it all.

For James Dickey

Sitting on a step unit going nowhere
On the theatre loading dock
Watching the red moon
Dying behind the artificial mists
After hearing Big Jim himself
The old night-fighter, Coke ad writer
Summon up a few ghosts
We all find within ourselves
Tuck, the bedtime hunter
And John the Baptist's honey-sweet, severed head
I scribble a few lines myself
Not in imitation, or search of glory
(My search is on a different stage)
But just to say, "Hey, Jim,
Amen!"

Sunrise in My Rearview Mirror

Sunrise in my rearview mirror
Naked mountains cutout against a spectrum sky
Somewhere distant a glowering cloud
        drops life on a mountain
In this old seabed, a cholla grows
A seamless land, pierced by rock ridges
        of earth's crusts
The sun chases me from ridge to ridge
Showing me their shades and colors
The sun is the grand killer here
Everything hides from it
We are in the Dead Mountains
Just south of the Valley of Death
(It's on the map, look it up)
By noon it will be fire here
But God and my Fiat willing
        I will be gone
Over the mountains to the sea
Past the dead and deadly beauty
Of this season of the sun.

December 8, 1980

Late-night company leaves me wondering
Were parting words an opening
      or a close
Did darkened words belie the
      glitter glance
Shall I call again
On another black and rainy night
Or am I fumbling in the dark
For a touch that isn't there

Far away, a singer died
You wanted to cry, but the newscaster
      thought too much
I wanted to comfort you
But the tears never cried

Don't you understand
I don't know what to do
Call me tomorrow
Drop an explicit hint
I know I am too old to be so young
But I am half Merlin and stand
      twisted in time

How can it be like this
The human race procreates
So not all stare question marks
      into the dark

I don't think too much, honest
I work at it
I just play his songs
But I wonder, at your fading back
How can I sing his songs
      to the empty sky.

Bourbon Street

Have you ever been to Bourbon Street
And seen the dancing girls
And wondered why
I have

I wondered why they danced
Then why we looked
Then I just wondered
Why?

The Last Generation

I am having trouble believing anything
Those of us of the Last Generation
Who face despair
About the time I was born
It became possible to kill everybody
In about thirty minutes
We've made it thirty years now
But the strain is beginning to show
Not long after came the silent Spring
Followed by the visible air, and other things
Little men calling themselves giant apes
Hammers and sickles, crescents and stars
Bloody crosses of every kind
Even beliefs that die-hard are killed
So, we grab for all the gusto
Because tomorrow, if there is one
Won't be as good
So you take what you can get
While it's there
And don't believe in anything
Cause that sucker will get us yet.

And Said So

Naked in bed
Reading the comics over her shoulders
(Doonesbury between her breasts)
As ways to begin a Sunday
I could think of worse
Later, slow love and pork chops
Soft thighs and tender loins
Supper by candlelight
Slow slide to tomorrow
On a day I fell in love

And said so.

Morning

I burned my hand
Taking the biscuits
Out of the oven
For the Sunday morning breakfast
After Saturday night love
She was cooking a cheese omelet
I made biscuits and coffee
We were not dressed
I think there will be a small scar
On my hand
Perhaps on my soul as well
For her love is hot
But, despite the danger
It is sometimes good
To warm one's hands
Near a fire.

Let This Be Said

Let this be said
In colder age or silent winter
I have been loved
And did also love
A woman fine and tender
In empty rooms or quiet halls
Mist naked trees or bitter breeze
If all my parchment crumble
For a span of days
In seasons hard or plenty
A woman fine saw me well in her eyes
And wept at the parting after.

Not Poetic

Desperation is not poetic
When three months out of work
One does not think of "checking account" as iambic
But as a beautiful girl
who vanished at the magician's wave
never to be seen again
Or as a lovely flower
that withered and died
There is no poetry
in an unemployment line
Just bare-light offices
with desk after desk
of unanswered whys
The very air is embarrassed
The counselors avoid your eyes
apologizing for having a job
One does not sing
on the way to the bottom
What lyrics go with moving out
but never moving in
What tune can you hum
while living off compassionate friends
Being unwanted, worthless
has no rhythm or rhyme
Dirges are for the dead
Blues for those alone
Desperation is not poetic
There are no songs
in the unemployment line.

Coach

I live with this cat, see
And on occasions, we hold these deep
      involved, complex, meow-filled conversations
That I never understand a word of
I'm not even sure what I'm saying
Not to mention him
Though usually, I think, he's trying to communicate
      some serious, long-held desire
For cheese, or love, or a good neck scratching
But I'm never sure, so I usually just scratch his back
And though I believe my enunciation
      in cat lingo is rather good
I get the impression he doesn't understand
      every meow I say
The result is usually less than serious failure
      to communicate
Though I guess it could be serious to the cat
      if he wants food
      and only gets his back scratched
My girlfriend occasionally imitates the cat
      when she wants her back scratched
But I suspect there's a bit more
      to that meow too.

Gridiron

It occurs to me
that nothing matters
except maybe football
maybe Alabama is right
and really crucial matters
are decided by linebackers
on lined fields of green
surrounded by a hundred thousand drunks
of one kind or another
those sober in blood
intoxicated by frenzy
or the delirium of a heavy bet
Tell me, Bear
who in felt fedora
walked on water
in posters and in Crimson hearts
Is this all that matters
that your valiant soldiers
win again their crusade
and again for honor and mother, win?
Will those of us who never
tread the numbered field
or cry with passion
for the winning score
never matter in this world
never find the open door
never be counted winners
never know the secret
of coming back
for the winning score?

Puff

I cannot sing
Puff the Magic Dragon
without crying
My eyes crack
my voice tears
After years and times
the effect remains
Childhood lost
brings weeping
But why?
I am not so old
as to foolishly long for youth
or so young
as to fear tomorrow
Other songs
grow old
and die
But Puff
roars yet
in my heart
Do I still long
for Hon-a-lee
or have I never
left it?

Waiting for the Mail

Waiting for the mail
Is like waiting for a new life
       to be born
One is sure something is coming
       sooner or later
But only god, not the poor man waiting,
       controls the time
And while one has some idea what to expect
       at least in outward form and shape
But no sure sign of the
       inner contents
So, postman or stork, are awaited
       nervously, in anticipation
Knowing one's fate, in little way or great,
       will change with the delivery.

Consuming Time

Nerves fray
Minds rot
TV, like a drug
Kills the senses
When overused
Abused
Used to deaden time
Time spent waiting
For a reason
Not to wait
Even books
Well written
Must be used
In moderation
Lest tolerance develop
To awe
While consuming time
Eating away life
While waiting
One must, as they say
(So right they are)
Do something
The fragile hours
Spent writing
Cannot support the day
It wants doing
It wants life
Outside the page
Duty done
Job completed
Love fulfilled
Beyond the paper glory
Beyond the silent page.

Fierce Freedom

It's the fierce freedom
I feel, walking alone
nibbling cookies fetched
from a bank contest table
The illusion of the open road
the solitary wanderer
living off the land
independent, his own man
Oh, that calls
Still
I was never that free
No road is really open
and my fate
has never been my own.

Saint Mary's Tears

In Nicaragua
they call the rain
Saint Mary's tears
Kathy, I'm crying too
But unlike your tears
which flow into my beard
as I hold you
mine flow inside my cheeks
under my skin
onto this paper
but I am just as sad
at leaving you
and my tears
are just as real
as Saint Mary's tears.

Songbook

In a songbook
borrowed from my sister
I found where she
in her adolescence
had scrawled her name
entwined with some teenage heartthrob
of Hollywood and fame
a new one for each page
sometimes just the name
of some overhyped, young girl's dreamboat
was enshrined alongside the title
of a pop-rock love tune
somehow associated with this lover-boy
but, toward the end,
in a section of almost forgotten oldies
in an innocent, unseeing wisdom
of future, longer days
her name alone was drawn
untied to plastic or electric sweetheart
beside an old, golden Dylan tune
about love being
just a four-letter word.

Dream

Did you ever see a dream disappear?
It is not a pretty thing
A cat paws
      at a golden ribbon
Then wonders where it has gone
      when it is jerked away
The cat forgets
      and moves on to other toys
But the dreamer's eyes gleam
      gold and green
Red with held-back tears
      turn white in disbelief
His ribbon was there
      scented with fame
Reeking of glory
      to hungry nostrils
Satin and lace
      to see and touch
The dreamer's hands
      like thumbless paws
Grasp lonely air
      the golden glory
Yanked away
      by an unseen hand
Replaced, perhaps,
      With pale, torn string
It is not a pretty thing.

Troubled

Troubled
Uncertain
Afraid
She gave
herself
to me
Such
Is
Love
Doubting
my love
Scorned
by another
Fearing
her womb
She gave herself
to me
Love
is such
Knowing
I would leave
Wary
of gossip
Seeing
no future
She gave
to me
herself
Such
love
is.

Suddenly Strange

It's strange to sleep alone
After waking up in a woman's room
Watching her dress
And eating her pancakes
With strawberry jam
It's strange to stick out my arm
And touch nothing
After kissing her in the park
Eating a picnic lunch
Chicken, fries, coleslaw
And a soft drink
It's strange how what was familiar
For thirty years
Can be suddenly strange
After so few nights
So few days
Of waking
In a woman's room.

Tanned

The ripe, golden apples of the sun
Shined above her blouse
Ready for plucking and tasting
Like an orchard just before harvest
Full and bountiful
The worms still hidden
Dry, wrinkled age
Still seasons away.

Send Not

I have spent too many afternoons
watching Dan Rather
explain bullet wounds
why should I, a Baptist
have to pray
for a pope
Because I know
those bells
toll for me
as much as any man
Each crazed slug
that strikes flesh
wounds me
with fear
and hate
And even if I
and whichever leader of fame
that falls
live to rise
It is peace
that dies.

Kentucky

The soft, blue mountains
hide such pain
the children clinging
to cloud fleece skirts
tied to her
by ignorance, fear
watching as she is raped
by strangers
fighting brothers, sisters
for the loose change
from the stranger's pockets.

You would not
let me love you.

State of Mississippi

Asshole of America
Ignorance glorified
So prejudiced they hate themselves
Land brown with black and white blood
Closed, out to lunch, forever
Forever afraid, forever poor
Forever Mississippi.

Hospital

From nursery Spring
To winter ICU
And all the Falls and Summers in between
Dr. Chronos carves our lives
Suturing the little cuts
But never staunching the flow
Of lifeblood
As patients come and go
Neonatal unit, hemo lab (Hymen's exam)
Emergency rooms and convalescent wards
Finally the coroner's cold table
From room to room we move
Ward to ward
Always dying
Always living our passing season
In sterile white
And artificial quiet.

In the Shower

Writing poetry
in the shower
is not easy
my habitual pen
is not on me
the only paper in reach
is not for writing on
I must remember a line
as I search for the next
while rubbing my head
with shampoo
remember, edit, create, wash
clean lines and wet hair
fearful some verse
will rinse from my head
and spin, gurgling
down the drain.

The Sound

The Sound! The Sound!
The Silence
Sounds in my ears
Drowns out thought
The throbbing quiet
Pounds my mind
An unheard scream echoes
Screeching, deafening
Ripping sanity
Crashing saneness
To tinkling bits
Trumpeted away
In the howling wind
Of silence.

Comparisons

Why can't I write like e.e.
But with capitals
Or solitary Emily
But without rhyme
Sing like Bonnie Bobby
But in American
Sound like Big Jim
But less macho
How did they get free
And not me?

I Never Had a Chance

I never had a chance
No choice was good
No choice was mine
One way sorrow
One way fear
No way open
No way near
Cry, sigh, or die
Face loneliness
Poverty, or tears
Flip the coin
Roll the die
Pay the dealer
The house always wins
You can't go home again
Not from this crap-shoot
This dunghill of life
Where living ain't easy
We're covered in sixes
So nobody wins
There aren't any odds
Nothing comes out even
When the dealer is
An unsmiling God.

Villanelle

Like sounds of hearts known never
        Passed over amid the throng
Such silence should be shunned forever

The lone, the flower plain, but clever
        Who sits by walls of song
Like sounds of hearts known never

The odd man out will one day sever
        A life that ends in endless wrong
Such silence should be shunned forever

So quiet, they say, a loner, why whoever
        Would have believed; an evensong
Like sounds of hearts known never

So passes pain, a life uncried, an endeavor
        Failed, a song that never could belong
Such silence should be shunned forever

And who shall sing, say I, and whatever
        Is my song is sad and long
Like sound of hearts known never
Such silence should be shunned forever.

Villanelle 2

Like little girls dancing naked in a stream
      Little joys of childhood disappear
Like little boys running barefoot in a dream

Innocence is not all it may seem
      But visions of it oftentimes appear
Like little girls dancing naked in a stream

To surprise our eye, a bit of youth redeem
      Both more and less, regret and fear
Like little boys running barefoot in a dream

I would not go back, crave candy and ice cream
      But rather wish such joy was near
Like little girls dancing naked in a stream

Big boys dream of girls' limbs that gleam
      Big girls of brazen men, the modern buccaneers
Like little boys, running barefoot in a dream

So time steals, none dance or dream
      And soon forget the memory clear
Of little girls dancing naked in a stream
Of little boys running barefoot in a dream.

Villanelle 3

A soul left alone to find his way
        A man gone cold in silence ice
For this there will be hell to pay

There is nothing as twisted, as hates the day
        Nothing for which there is a higher price
As a soul left alone to find his way

Someone sans softness, no word to say
        No memory of tender, no knowledge of nice
For this, there will be hell to pay

Who do we blame, guilt at what feet lay
        When all passed by, not thinking twice
A soul left alone to find his way

To you, I say, who would not stay
        Who gifts of love considered vice
For this there will be hell to pay

There will be blood, in time there may
        Be tears, as to him are passed God's dice
A soul left alone to find his way
For this there will be hell to pay.

Doing Sit-ups

Doing sit-ups
on the floor
in the morning
my cat watches me
thinking
he owns
a curious
human.

July 4, 1985, Atlanta

Morning street lined with wives, children, friends
cheering the tailenders
who jog and smile and wave
running for T-shirts and joy

Afternoon we stand above the raining street
sheltered by parking garage level four
and are attacked by thousands of red balloons
loosed to signal the parade
the wind whips the balloons under our roof
as we scamper and laugh for joy

Evening waiting, waiting in rain for dark
to blaze the sky with fire and flame
under the umbrella we wow and ah
red, green, yellow, blue showers overhead
spins, wheels, bursts, burns, and falls
changing to water that splashes at our feet
changing thunder and lightning into bolts of joy.

Little Tragedies

Little tragedies produced but unreviewed
The wails heard only by the broken soul
Our lives play tearfully to empty houses

There is silence in the wings
As we fret our hour on the stage
Without prompt or stage directions

Only the ghost of the boards
Sees our all-too-common show
Hears our oft-echoed lines in silence

There will be no applause, no bow
When rings the curtain down
We took our role as cast

Remembered our lines, hit our marks
And made our exits
Without bumping into the furniture

Alas, poor Yorick, no one knew him well
Soliloquies and monologues
We are such stuff, till only pages

Are left, yellowing, turning to dust
Lost manuscripts
Of ill-remembered plays.

The Crystal Thought

There is virtue in simplicity
The diamond is not complex
only pure
The crystal thought
or sparkling image
Outshines the multi-strata stone.

April, Mississippi

Green Spring
hippity heat
soul-searing sun
Ford sauna
melting across wet asphalt
riding rails over shrunken rivers
(no starch, please)
let it hang limp
hair does today
tongues too
panting steam
no A/C in poverty/outdoors
just sweat
a season ahead of the calendar
Delta down here
digging, dying
rotting unborn
cotton wet and dry
wait until July
then it really gets hot.

In the *New Yorker*

In the *New Yorker* poetry of mine
just will not fit. No such sophisticate
am I. I'm just a Southern boy, unversed
in city life, so very unrehearsed
for talk o're teacups bone and delicate,
for references to artists Florentine.
So too for Poetry, the holy shrine
of densest verse, that claims to hold the state
of printing best in form and thought, so first
the poet's reputation comes, who nursed
the rhymes till thirst and mind the lines do sate.
I'm hungry still, but pen will not resign.

The Sprinter

My feet are latex
Near naked I stand
            and kneel
            and fly
        at the flash of the shot
trying to touch the golden strand
        before the sound has died.

I Sometimes Wonder

I sometimes wonder
why we consider
the soft, virgin snowfall
a symbol
of innocence and purity
when each white snowflake
requires a sooty speck of sin
about which to crystalize
its life.

Whenever the Morning Newspaper

Whenever the morning newspaper
Is not on the lawn
I wonder if the world is ending
And the reporters found out
And went home
Rather than bannering the news
Like a cartoon prophet
Leaving the rest of us
To face the end
Unknowing
Over cereal or donuts.

There's a Difference

There's a difference between
The way old lovers touch
And the eager new
There's no exploring
They know
How to cup the hand
To fit the breast
As natural as a football
In a wide receiver's soft hands
As welcome as old friends
On a Sunday afternoon.

Proposal to Kathy

Consider me
A la Al Jolson
On my knee
Singing I love you
Singing the song
I never sang
To one girl before
Let me sing

Come, woman of joy
Be my wife
Let us burn our passions together
Till time makes us old friends
Who warm each other's lives
As the world grows cold

Let me sing your glory
Let me lie in your arms
    when you laugh
Let me hold you in my arms
    when you cry
Let me lie down beside you
    in the dark lonely night
Let me dance with you
    in the bright shining day
Let us eat together
    the chocolate candy happiness
Let us drink together
    the castor oil pain
Let us give birth to flowers

Let us buy a five-dollar license
That comes with no guarantees

Only promises
I promise you
That love will grow
Will ebb and flow
That we, and life, will change
Life is change
Alone or together
God grant we ride the wave of time
Together

God did not promise me tomorrow
Nor grant me second sight
I can guarantee nothing
But today's love
But if my little wisdom
Tells me anything
It is that
I want you
      near me
      beside me
      touching me
      singing me
      loving me
And I you
And that will be good
    and bad
Easy, and hard
Spring, and Winter

I am wise enough to know
I know little
I know this
I want
Like a guitar wants music
Or paper, words

For us
To be friends and lovers
To touch and to cling
In light and in dark
In sorrow and in joy
In glory and in shame
In heyday and in disaster
In boredom and in delight
In ecstasy and in pain
To give gladly body and mind
To respect and trust
To merge our lives into a single stream
Flowing through the hills and valleys of life
As long as the grass grows
And the rivers run

Send me your song
Send me your dance
Send me your yes.

The Wind Is Singing

Outside my thermo-pane
double-glass, insolated window
the wind is singing
I can tell because
the tree limbs are keeping time
the tune is unheard
beneath the rush
of air conditioner fan
the roar of I-285 traffic
the thunder of planes headed for Hartsfield
and the beep of a backing truck
this mechanized chamber group
does not play Brahms
or even Ives
no wonder then
the waterfall has fallen
out of modern music
no brook babbles on the radio
Windsong is a perfume
not a top-forty tune
we sing what we hear
we do not hear
the melody of leaves.

I-285, Seven a.m.

The red/white snake
scraped across dawn
doing sixty, sixty-five, more
in a loop
those on her back
rode the ride
slowly poisoned each other
or bit with metal fangs
then circled back
each evening
(when the stripes reversed)
and ended up
going nowhere.

You Can't

You can't write about silence
it doesn't move
it has no color
your own screams cannot break it
it stands
like a prison guard on watch
it burns
like an ulcer, slow and steady
you can't even listen for it
it creeps
like fog on a black night
it stings
like a thousand fleas
you can't even die from it
and that becomes your greatest fear
that it will follow you beyond the grave.

Tammy and Jim

Tammy and Jim
it's such a surprise
to learn you're a doper
and a screwer of men
We'd never have guessed
though Amiee Simple knew
away in Mexico
with you know who
And Minister Billy Jim
(remember him?)
who said the vows
for those he knew
(biblically, both women and men)
suspected at least
But they're forgotten
since never TV'ed
so we're surprised
by pills and whores
But the sin is ours
for forgetting the past
for accepting words
for believing in men.

No More Time

There's no more time for the green songs
sung by the woodfire cold and gray
for the glories of the green hill
now red and brown. Life falls away.

No more time for the Indian wind
of chilling cheeks and crystal skies
for cricket tunes or fresh-made pies
not from a can. Life falls away.

And in our rush to coldness, o're crackling leaves
dropped dead before us, past greener
passion times when sap ran strong
let once again the breeze strum
our stiffened limbs in one more
warm wild song, before life falls away.

The Pin-up

What were you thinking
When you posed
With hands on hips
Bathing suit pulled down
Below your breasts
Were you thinking of the money
Or how good it was to be beautiful
Or how sexy it felt to reveal yourself
Or of the hot lights and stiff muscles
Or that you were not a person
Only a picture
Did you think of young boys
And lonely old men
Playing with themselves
As they stared at your image
And did that please you
Did you ever think of me
Sitting at my desk
Wondering who you are
Where you come from
Why you did it
What you were thinking
When you posed?

Fast Food

If Ronald McDonald
clown that he is
married Mrs. Winner
for her coleslaw
would they have
little baby chicken burgers
or would it be a sterile marriage
because of fat in the tubes?
Or if Colonel Sanders
the old lecher
seduced young Wendy
with his large-size fries
would she bear him
seven secret herbs and spices
then demand child support
or wrap them in a sesame seed bun
and carry them home?

Challenger

Seven ashes to four winds
to scattered bodies go
Roger, throttle up
104 percent of max
and then, beyond
scattered ashes go
The Face of God
fills the screens
Roger, throttle up
beyond the max
Houston, do you copy?
the stars have changed
Do you copy, Houston?
it's a new sky
Houston, do you copy?
All systems go at throttle up
Roger, Challenger
This is Gus at CapCom
You're go for high orbit
Gus?
Yeah?
Hell of a ride
Roger that
Roger, go for high orbit
Throttle up.

The Gate

My father is a gate guard now, he works
outside a mill. His post a shack of brick
and glass inside a wire fence. It irks
me sore to know his twilight tears some trick
of fate has set. I see him yet in times
gone by, in Sunday shoes, in coat and tie,
in pulpit standing, Bible by, with rhymes
and verses preaching, teaching, all a sigh
o're sins and follies mortal, of men and grace,
of God on high, of faith and Jesus Christ.
He wore God's glory then, it filled the space
around his feet of clay. It's gone, a heist
of time. A fallen soul remains within the wall
to guard a lower gate, await a higher call.

The Maya

The Maya
who ripped the beating heart
from the chest of the human sacrifice
thought
he was pleasing God

The Inquisitor
who thrust the burning iron
into the flesh of the heretic
thought
he was defending God's Word

The Pharisee
who paid the crowd
to cry "Crucify, Crucify!"
thought
he was saving God's Nation

I fear
somewhere
another holy man
is thinking.

When Writing

When writing poetry
always double space
between the lines
It's a clue
as to where
the real poetry
lies.

To Say I Love

How many ways
to say I love
with words of course
gentle touch, sex
the glance or gift
poem, child, home
time, concern, care
kiss, caress, calm
tears, years
till no question
no doubt
just knowing
eases the long night.

Test

I see skulls
in the flower print
of the bedspread
and wonder
if the anonymous artist
deliberately concealed
death heads
in the greenery
as some macabre joke
on unwary sleepers
or if it's me
my unique perspective
of inkblots or daises
that stares back at me
through empty sockets
a mirror
of my mind.

9/9/89

toward the last
when the mind thought
the sodden limbs
were chained
you remembered
exactly where
the crowbar was
left corner of the garage
behind the trash cans
but none of your beloved tools
lined so carefully
along the workshop wall
could break these bonds
age, cancer, pressured heart
and the two women
who cared for you
could only laugh
eighty-two
too weak to move
wanting a crowbar
to pry off death.

Dead Yet

"Am I dead yet?"
The old man asked
In sane delirium
"Did the cancer get me?"
No regret
Just curiosity
"Have the funeral notices gone out?"
Inhabiting another world
He faced reality

The doctor
Unprepared for such eternity
Had no answer.

Squirrels

drink from the birdbath
and eat the sunflower seeds
the birds drop
from the feeder
they hide nuts
among the leaves
and shiver
when the breeze
foretells the time to come
they climb the tree
fold their little paws
and chatter
to the squirrel god
praying
for mild winds
and clumsy birds

And from my own
square, wooden nest
I watch the leaves fall
consider fire and ice
and whisper
Amen.

The Congregation

The congregation
of mourning doves
on the birdbath
make their absolution
sip the sacramental pool
and wing to heaven
like prayers of fools.

What I'm Writing

I don't like what I'm writing these days
too much ice this winter
but dry, no gleaming snow with soft edges
just cold, hard, and silent
like writing with a knife.

God's Millstone

God's millstone grinds on
ignorant of the corn
that yesterday
reached for the sun

time's water turns the wheel
and flows on
never knowing the stone
white as bone

heaven's rain, far away
falls on the mountain
unaware that down the stream
it will power the wheel

and in earth's field
the broken stalk
dries and dies
bereft of golden grain.

Turning Away

Turning away
like a woman in bed
who wants to sleep
leaving me
to slowly chill
body heat ebbing away
one day you will cover me again
with earth and grass
and I, in the darkness
will remember
your turning away.

Life

Life
a sexually transmitted disease
ultimately fatal
with no known cure
or treatment
characterized
by gradual destruction of the body
long-term, low-grade pain
with occasional episodes
of spontaneous remission
usually not long-lasting
there are some antidotal cases of survival
but none are scientifically documented
it is highly infectious during intercourse
but otherwise difficult to transmit
the only known preventative is education
but even that is not highly effective
treatment is symptomatic
just make the poor bastards
as comfortable as you can
until it's over.

In Kentucky

In Kentucky
winter strips the land
revealing its barren skin
pox-marked, bruised
until the snow
like a vice cop
covers the naked sin.

At Night

At night
I wake
straining
to hear
amplified
breathing
from the
next room
trying
to distinguish
my wife's snores
from the electric
baby breaths
whose silence
awakens me
in terror.

Elizabeth's Eyes

The eyes are mine
the nose, cheeks, etc.
are from her mother
but the eyes are mine
and she haunts me
staring back at me
with my eyes
how much of me
can she see
with my eyes?

According to Regulations

According to the regulations
life should be typed
double spaced
in 10 pt. Courier
on 20 lb. paper
but somehow
Helvetica 30 pt. bold
keeps breaking out
on my printer.

The Words

The old poetic tricks don't work today
Sonnets just do not fit the times
The bards of old who sang a lay
Can't rock and roll or rap their lines
So Poe and Pope are 'round the bend
Compared to Guns N' Roses, Grateful Dead
Don't count iambs, don't even pretend
To care how strong stress is said
Count quarter time and beats to the bar
Top forty airplay, concert gross
To find the latest shooting star
Who thinks image, not words, is boss

And bless Paul Simon, Diamond, Byrds
Dylan, Lennon, and Cohen
For they remember words.

The Turned Phrase

The turned phrase
turns on me
reflecting back
a darker eye

These days
just walking
takes effort
I used to flow
effortlessly
from hill
to hill
scene
to scene
now I watch
children run
as aimless
as my gaze

The T-shirt
on the actor
said
"My youth,
which way
did it go?"
It went
that-a-way
where time,
unlike a phrase,
never turns.

An Art

There is an art
to living tired
to waking up
while still asleep
to sleeping awake
to dying slowly
long day
by short night.

Always Away

Elizabeth
you are doing very well
being cute for Mommy
growing too fast for her
claiming yourself
with little grasping hands
eating the world
edible or not
today you crawl
tomorrow you run
always away
always away.

My Daughter's First Vomiting

Her look said
what the hell is this
as vomit poured out
her nose and mouth
this is no milk spit-up
what is happening to me
are my insides coming out
does this happen often
is this growing up
why is this happening
what do I do now?

I changed the bed
Mommy changed the clothes
Life is full of little changes.

Proper Nouns

Decisions are made quietly
in empty rooms
by proper nouns
Verbs may spring the doors
daunt the trees
careen outside
be criticized
by adverb clowns
but decisions
are made quietly
in empty rooms
by proper nouns.

Lost Persona

Shredded paper
wadded up
tossed away
into the gutter
gets rained on
coagulates
into a lump
of dyed cellulose
decomposes
rots
and dies

the words
it held
unknown
forever lost.

The Pool

The bronze bikini girls bake
by the pool beside my apartment
asses or tits thrust upward
barely covered from burning sun.
No one swims.
It is an exercise of burning youth
to ashes of soft bodies and hard skins.
They bask in burnished glory,
posing as I stroll by,
musing of even barer bodies
in the faceless sex of dreams,
the eternal fantasy of undeserved love.
The nightmare stares us in the face.
They are burning for beauty
and the blessings beauty brings.
I am burning for dreams
that bless the dreamer
before only ashes
are left to sing.

Eyes

There are no horrors left
the Holocaust, Cambodia
Kennedy, King, wounded Wallace, Pope
boned Ethiopia, wired Argentina
even Hiroshima, Nagasaki ashes
Palestine sells fear for dimes
Mother Russia gulags her sons
and petty men bleed petty crimes
scared inhabits modern eyes
but horror is defunct
roaches will inherit, maybe ants
buttons can be pushed
eyes sliced open clean
the womb can feel a jagged edge
babies fed to bees
horror comes only from surprise
that such a thing can be
what eyes my eyes have seen
know such a thing could be.

Sunny Lines

I sit inside on summer days
and try to think of sunny lines
that rhyme or rhythm set
or freer verse by reason so declined
in warmer climes however
often thunderclouds darken view
metaphors thunder rather than shine
similes strike, not glow
so versed in storm am I
of cloud tears running rivulets down
of rushing, chilling, windy themes
that even on burning, blueish days
beyond the horizon
my eyes see gathering, grayish clouds.

So Caesar Said

The Druids, so Caesar said
sacrificed their mortal foes
in wooden cages of flesh and flame
to stately oaks and balls of mistletoe
he thought that not quite right
but he was sliced to bits
on sacred ground in Senate hall
by friends and fellow countrymen
who prayed on Power's lowly alter
so Caesar had no right to talk.

Christmas Vision

It was Christmas
the afternoon lull
past presents
and filling meal
I sat to watch some ballgame
my mother lay on the couch
to nap
during some aftershave ad
I glanced at her
Death had touched her face
she lay, arms crossed
as if . . .
This is how
she will look
I thought
when . . .
face sagged smooth
still
gone
resting in the arms of . . .
a nap
for her
I will be the one
who stares into the face

the rise and fall
of her stomach
reassured me
but the image
remains
Age and Time

new fears
now named.

Birth

Black life crawls out
draining dreams
Death of birth
Birth of death
Passing a torch
of pain
Is any man as guilty
as when he condemns
his own son to life
and himself
to fading
for another
Death drives us to birth
Better we quietly die
than infect another soul
There is no purgatory
only life
That is hell enough
Why inflict it
on another
and call it love?

New Life

An awesome thing, new life, from penis to
the cervix, up the tube to ovary
and back again in pain to giggles, goos
to toddler, tot, and off to school
then dates, hot nights, and wedding vows
and one more song of sex as sperm to ovum go
again, same song, second verse, granddad, grandson
grand time was had by all, so small a note
discordant sounds amid the chorus loud
A god was wise it seems to make the penis blind
and hide the cervix in a darkened room
too much pain shines beyond
so those who live by eyes would never shout
Encore! Encore! but quietly and one
by one at intermission fade.

Choices

You don't get many choices in this life
and most are devil or the deep blue sea,
of rocks or places hard, of frying pans or fires,
of wife's too-frozen silence or a baby's squalls
no music here, no jigs or squares to call
us from toil. Bitter tastes, garlic tears,
attic odors, the poor man's faded sight.
Choose, choose! blind canyons, darker caves,
tigers behind every door, wearing veils and curls
the eaten man may cry a warning
but the dark pit is irresistible
We all go in to win the princess
Never remembering the year-king
Never remembering that the fertility god
has to die.

Geometry

Euclid believed in flat

Pythagoras believed in
                right
              angles

Descartes was
for   grids

              time
  Einstein
                      relative
      space
          as
  saw

August

It is August
the leaves in my driveway yellow are
dry and brittle
doomed to sight
a dry year
when leaves die
before the season turns
pleasant, stable
the weather was
sunny and warm
fine future forecast
day after day
a regular paycheck
so dependable, secure
count on established, steady days
warm sun, cloudless blue
umbrella dusty, forgotten
in easy, sunny Summer
until it August is
and the leaves
in my driveway
yellow are.

Ease Him Gently

Ease him gently into life
my son or daughter
who to be
Life begins in pain and tears
and ends the same
a light beginning let it be
and end the same
and in between
though much the same
may they remember this
a bright beginning we begot
as best we could, a kiss
a prayer, a hope for this
they would be glad we beginning gave
before into the mist we fade.

The Addicted

In my unsmoking office
the addicted
hide in the aptly named firestairs
like schoolgirls
sneaking to the john
to consume a bite of forbidden, tasty death
grown men and women
with MAs and Maseratis
huddle together
on stone steps
littered with their own ashes
medicated by ether
bound by brownish leaves
self-respect their victim
they grovel on the stone.

Not Quite

Computer keyboard clicks
      crunch not like leaves
Forced air circulation
      sings not like breeze
Elevator signal rings
      are not larksong
Telephones buzz
      but not like bees
Even glowing lights
      Are not the sun
So denizens of office deeps
      are not quite men.

Soho

Soho like a signal lays
not far from mighty Thames
and Donavan, whose deed is done
is now a singing hymns
farther down the path
Mick's turned gray
Herman's trying opera
Dave Clarks only one again
here and there a gravestone head
a Jim, a John
a time, a day, passed away
Strawberry Fields forever.

Seasons

Caress me a spring flower
that wakes, sparkles to bees
and in soaks the sun
before its day departs
Kiss me suddenly summer
warm and wet and wild
smiling some old psalm
of seasons sliding into years
On me gently fall
turning to me in the sunset
as tree to earth returns
in the passing of the tears
Embrace me warmly as winter fire
wearing flames in hearthstone hues
finding fine fierce surgings
through darkest eves in times to end.

Poetry

Nothing rhymes with orange
Except perhaps door hinge
Even worse is rhyming month
Without a lisping once
So never sing of girls named Ann
And forever let there be a ban
On sonnets that dare begin
"As I was eating my Ann's juicy orange
It came to me I love Ann and this month."

So go from there if you can
But don't blame me if you don't understand
That poetic suicide is a venal sin.

Twenty Years

Twenty years
after my cat has died
I will still be finding
cat hairs
on my
clothes.

See This

See this?
Want to see it again?
Watch closely now.
There!
Did you see it?
Did you see the world end?
Or do you want me
To do it again?

Damn Cute

You better be damn cute
That's all I can say
You better be damn cute
To take all my money
       my time
       my sleep
       my life
The minute the doc said yes
I had to start hustling
       moonlighting
       pinching
And you no bigger than a pinhead
Everybody's happy but me
I'm just tired
Maybe sick
Certainly scared
So you better be damn cute.

In the February

In the February
white and brittle
new life blows
reds and purples
In the October
Life will turn
Again to winter
Browns and grays
A cycle
so they say
the endless mystery
of life
What is never spoken
is the pain
of the broken limb
The aged, twisted tree
seeing the acorn
who has never known the lightning
      heard the thunder
      felt the hail
      bent the wind
      burned the sun
Sprout
thinking only May
never dreaming December.

I Like to See You Naked

I like to see you naked
Sitting at the breakfast table
Eating Corn Chex
It seems so healthy.

I Will Sing

Yes, I will sing
but
a sad song
a blues, perhaps
but without the rage
softly, without feeling
a hurt long gone
from another day
a little jazz echo
behind a lone guitar
six strings
plastic
imitation guts
hollow inside
to swell the sound
with sympathetic vibrations
can you hear it cry?
like the wind
from a train
long gone
just missed.

Oedipus Eyes

We had
Vietnam for breakfast
The Killing Fields for lunch
The Sudan for dinner
For snacks
We ate Hinkley
And Speck
At midnight
A bite of Bundy
Before sleep
Cast iron stomachs
No Pepto in sight
If it bleeds
It leads
And poor poets
Stare at Oedipus eyes
That have seen too much
And will not blink.

What Gets Said

Did you ever wonder
what gets said
in the dressing room
of a strip club
Do the dancers
as they attire
for disrobing
count the house
Are men disparaged
in crude, vile terms
or evaluated
based on wallet size
Perhaps it's just
another kind of office
full of gossip, cookies
and pictures of kids
Is there shop talk of
a new way to shake it
or envy of the new kid
not yet on a diet
Do they ever
talk of sex
or is that taboo
among the nude?

Too Young

I am too young
to be reading obituaries
in newspapers, professional journals
and alumni newsletters
we should be dying
in car crashes
to everyone's surprise
not of pneumonia
as expected
but the black of ink
confirms
what is under the lines
we are losing ourselves
too soon
too soon.

Biopsy

Mortality struck at four o'clock
by phone
a little brown freckle
renamed carcinoma
under the microscope
called to say
you too shall pass
do not count your years
until the candles are on the cake
that little girl
may grow up without you
retirement may never come
enjoy the rosebuds
while they bloom
come back Thursday at two
and we will cut you.

Generations

Watching my mother and daughter
      clearing the dinner table
Time, defying Einstein
      summersaults
I see my mother young
      my daughter old
My mother is twenty-five again
      near the end of the war
Newly married, happy
      in Oklahoma
Not bent by ill children
      and a difficult man
My daughter is also twenty-five
      suddenly mature
Beautiful, but with sad eyes
      having seen too much
Wondering what loads
      will weigh her down
And I stand between
      seeing both visions
Eyes wet for what was
      and what will be.

Parenthood

Parenthood opposes poetry
clear lines leap not from hazy minds
that seek lost sleep in quiet times
that once filled brains with energy

"Diaper" and "potty" fit no refrain
though tiny hands and hugs inspire
though cute the curl or soft the smile
out of baby's reach, my pen is lain

So cuddle on my lap, my love
it's Mother Goose's time to shine
so ask not from my treasure trove
for Daddy's out of rhyme.

Seeing My Daughter

Seeing my daughter silhouetted against the window
As she watched the leaves fall on the porch roof below
I, corny as it seems, thought about the falling days
My days turning gold or brown, hers only budding
But all falling away in the chilling wind.

Elizabeth

Laughter chasing bubbles
      in the wind

Joy catching a ball
      in outstretched hand

Peace sleeping quietly
      in my arms.

Coach, a Cat

There's no time for crying
not even for kitty cats
that a little girl kissed
and snuggled like a pillow
but lost to sleep
like a memory
of toddler times
fading through the years.

Hardly-A-Ford

Howdy, folks
Tom Hardly here, for Hardly-A-Ford
If you're a red-blooded American
you want an American car
not something built by a bunch of Japs or Huns
no matter how good it is
Well, up here at Hardly-A-Ford
we've got real American cars
      built by real American nigras
      up in Detroit
We're located up here in the mountains
      where our heads are low
      and everything's cheap
So come see us at Christmas
      when we're all lit up
And remember, if you're going to do it
      do it to the Hardly boys.

BC

PC crash? That's a BC headache
WC won't flush? That's a BC headache
Head hurts so bad you can't see?
      Take BC
In pain from listening to me?
      Take BC
BC headache powders
Tastes so bad
You forget your head.

Black Pavement

Black pavement
white mists
dead rain
rising
to meet
its maker.

Hey, Kids

Hey, kids
    Home from school?
    Want to play around a little
        but not get caught?
Get new Kiddie Condoms
    Specially made for growing boys and girls
Packaged to look just like bubble gum
    Kiddie Condoms
In the toy section of your drugstore
    Kiddie Condoms
Get yours now.

To Elizabeth, before Her Birth

I have started watching
      the little girls
           before church
Wondering if you
      will sit quietly
           in frilly dress
Or scamper off
      to kick around
           with the boys
What will your smile be like?
Your hair, short or long?
Will you hug my leg
      as some girls
           do their fathers
Will your eyes sparkle
      blue or brown
           under bangs
Will you really love
      a bald old man
           with sad eyes?

My Father

My father
is dying
a little faster
than the rest of us

Sharp knives
and long
chemical poisons
only slow the black dancer

His whole life
he did everything
deliberately, perfectly
no matter how long it took

I suspect
he will deal
with dying
the same.

Blood is Red

If the blood is red
life is a problem
blood, sweat, or tears
we are born in blood
we sweat through life
we die in tears
and in between
the blood is red
the sweat is hot
the tears are mean.

Elizabeth

Elizabeth, can you feel it
when I rub your mother's tummy?
Is that harder area
below her navel your head?
Is my hand there at all
or do you swim unaware
that someone, somewhere
wants to calm you
the only way he knows how.

Little Things

I have a little list
of little things to do
and one by one
each little thing
I make each one come true
and in a little while
I look back at my little list
and see how many little things
combine just bit by bit
to make a little life.

The Baby

The baby on the other side of the glass
its life still measured in minutes
opens its salved eyes
and stares at me
asking
where am I
what have you done to me
what did I do to deserve this?

Jim and Tammy

Jim and Tammy
had a show
that sold a cross
for a billion gross
so Praise the Lord
and pass the yacht
come ride the waterslide
just send in seventy-five
So Tammy got high
but wouldn't go down
on Jim so Jessie did
then tarts and Joes
what a life
take my wife
cue the condominium
Keep those checks coming in
There's blackmail to pay
poor in Palm Springs to help
pantyhose to sell
timeshare with Jesus, $5000 down
Curse those sinners
Get rich as a bitch
Live like there ain't no hell
Isn't religion wonderful?

To the Tune Of

Oral, Oral, are you praying
are you praying in the tower
in the tower? A sixty-foot-high Jesus
yes, a sixty-foot-high Jesus
wants you dead, wants you dead
better raise some money
better raise some money
'bout eight mil, 'bout eight mil
Oral, Oral, are you fasting
are you fasting between meals
between meals? Have them send the money
yes, have them send the money
save your soul, save your soul
better ask for mercy
better ask for mercy
you'll go to hell, go to hell.

Communication

And it's, like, well, OK, you know?
so I said, all right, like, see?
but she said, uh, no, like, well, you know?
OK, OK, I said, like, fine, sure.
You just, like, you know, don't get me,
and I'm, like, talking, you know,
so, OK, like, it's not my, you know, fault
if you can't, like, understand, you know?

Missing

Do you see this?
Of course not.
   isn't there.

Disney World

Even in Disney World
Every day's the same
Only the tourists change
Micky and Goofy
Change insides frequently
For after five thousand boat rides
Adventureland isn't an
Fantasyland loses its
Tomorrowland has one too many yesterdays
And nobody really lives in Epcot
    (despite the name).

Pegasus

Pegasus
old prom date
who jerked drugstore sodas in Arizona
has disappeared
into time's sea
even the soda fountain is gone
like Arizona's ocean
only the beach remains
I remember her
but she is gone
flown over the moon
on white wings
young and graceful
to never-never land
never to return
Still
like youth
she haunts me
like all missed chances
like all myths
when we believed what the gods said
when we believed
So
my flying horse
of teenage dreams
wherever you are
I wish you well
and wonder
if you remember me
as some lost
misguided
Apollo.

In Middle Age

In middle age
the world cools
wives forbid hot women
so ends the chase
jobs become jobs
not career prospects
novelty becomes impossible
dreams get stale
you have what you have
you are what you are
and if the blood is slower
it is not you becoming older
it is a world gone cold.

Dear Sir

The answer to your question
No
You can't
You won't
It's not allowed
It's immoral
It's illegal
It's not the custom
Mother wouldn't like it
Somebody might object
It might corrupt the kids
It's offensive
It's obscene
It's not polite
And I wouldn't like it
So don't you dare
Or I'll blow your fucking brains out
With my god-dammed thirty-eight.

Milk Cartons

The silent door
answers the knock

Visions of fat cops
in triplicate
dance in my head

Missing heartaches
on milk cartons.

Words

            words
           are like
         bricks that you
        stack one on another
      until you have constructed an
    edifice reaching to the gods above.

On the Day

On the day that Ruby shot Oswald
I was thirteen years old
and visiting a friend's dairy farm
I saw a cow moaning over her calf
stiff-legged on the ground
looking through the fence
at eyes big with death
I saw I did not understand
but knew I would see it over and over
until I learned.

Light

If, in this pause in the jackhammer
I had something significant to say
I would not feel the silence lost
But my mind, like the sky, is empty
The everyday light hiding
The blazing stars beyond.

One Night

One night
and maybe soon
the phone will ring
a death
tears
an unsmiling airplane
as she
or I
to mother
or father
fly
to say words
make arrangements
and cry
ashes, dust
a cold day in July
an empty place
a long goodbye
and then
a fear
of phones
of nights
that cry.

AIDS

Acquired
Immune
Deficiency
Syndrome
Attacks
Hearts
Hardening
Solidifying
Among
Uninfected
Fear.

A Living

William Carlos Williams
was a doctor
Charles Ives
sold insurance
Lawrence Ferlinghetti
    sells books
Nobody
lives on songs
No matter how
wonderful the tune.

Bloody Lines

easy, bloody lines
nothing obtuse
or referential
just sliced veins
raw nerves
guts on the floor

poetry.

Exploratory Haiku

They opened him up
        took one look and sewed him up
                after seeing no hope.

The Vase

The vase sat on the shelf
dusty
designed to hold beauty
and life
it stood empty
the hardened clay
developing minute cracks
it wanted use
else one day
a shattering
even as it sat.

Question

What's on the inside side
of a belly belly button?
Does an innie stick out
and an outie go in?
What's left of whatever was there
when it led from dear old mother to where?
The outside side was cut and clamped,
knotted or tied
Till a baby belly button bloomed
astride our front side
But the inside side was left alone
with the other muscle and bone
So what was there did what it liked,
as we made mudpies or rode our trikes
Leaving me wondering, as gentlemen do,
of kites and skies, of wheres and whys,
Of uncles and hymns, of do or dies,
of belly belly button inside sides.

Villanelle for a Cat

Even the cat is mad at me
And stares me down with hungry eye
Because it's feeding time, you see

Because he will not pay his fee
And I'm content to let him lie
Even the cat is mad at me

All I charge for dinner and tea's
A moment's petting on my thigh
Before it's feeding time, you see

But not so low his dignity
To such he will not mollify
Even the cat is mad at me

Soon the case will reach perigee
One of us must eat humble pie
Because it's feeding time, you see

PhD versus pedigree
And I've no need to wonder why
Even the cat is mad at me
Because it's feeding time, you see.

He and I

The unknown Portuguese sailor
whose portrait hangs on my wall
was visiting Boston on a sunny day
and happened to catch an artist's eye
a moment's repose
as pastels flew
then he was gone
to crowds or sea or foreign land
then an artist's gift to a friend
my marriage to her
and the Iberian brown eyes
from the slightly tilted head
stare down at those below
leaving us to wonder, he and I
what sees or is seen
and where and why
the eyes, the eyes, the eyes.

Writers

The famous Southern poet
now old, writes, they say
two hours a day
the jockey-turned-mystery
writer goes for six
on yellow legal pads
while staring at the sea
the Hollywood female
of scandal/romance fame
went for ten or twenty
in bursts of weeks
till done or exhausted
(she's dead)

There are those
who live to write
and those
who write to live
and many
somewhere in between

But how much is said
and how much worth saying
and who says it best
is not an hours test.

Good Sense

Nonsense rhymes with horsesense
And horsesense is oxymoronic
So horsesense is nonsense
But not recipricalic
For nonsense can make sense
An amazing, wonderful trick
Which makes no sense
at all.

Writing

Writing is easy
Selling is hard
Xeroxes and stamps
S.A.S.E., rejection slips
Blood, sweat, tears
Faceless names
Nameless faces
"We regret to inform . . ."
"There were many considerations"
"We received 2947 submissions"
"Please keep us in mind"
"We are no longer reading . . ."
"Return to sender, delivery refused"

Writing is easy
Selling is hard.

By the Time

By the time the call comes
no one will answer
no one will be left
just a shuck of dry-year corn
we have a job for you
they will want to say
but it will be too late
the man will be gone
something may pick up the phone
maybe even say yes
hollow yes, echo yes, empty yes
yes too late, after no no no no
"He who lives on hope dies farting"
if no then no why no so no
no, no, no, no, no
the silent telephone
the empty mailbox
the dry days months years
even the Arizona frogs
who dormant go till water
or desert seeds that lie years till rain
if no rain, if no water, if no
then one day the limit will pass
no yes then will bloom the dry seed
no yes then will stir the empty egg
no yes then will save the gone soul
no yes then will be answered
by more than hollow man
by more than echo no.

To Write

To write
you have
to think

That makes
it hard

To write
you have
to feel

That makes
it hurt

To write
you have
to know

That makes
it impossible.

Church

Through the glass darkly I stare
Far away a bell tolls
The sound is silence
Someone cries an empty tear

The churches are full
       of empty people

Lo, I am with you
       not peace but a sword

The stained glass bleeds
The choir is hired
Ah, look at all the lonely
From here they do come from.

Villanelle

I do not want to write a villanelle
They're just too hard, too much a rhyming trick
I wish that I could somehow break their spell

Some poets can dash them off pell-mell
I waddle on through words molasses thick
I do not want to write a villanelle

The rhymes have but a two-tone knell
That rings like childish, obscene limerick
I wish that I could somehow break their spell

A bad one smells like long-dead mackerel
A good one reads like formal rhetoric
I do not want to write a villanelle

Obsessed by this, a literary muscatel
A maverick, love-sick, drunken lunatic
I wish that I could somehow break their spell

I'm in a kind of minor poet's hell
To think that this would be my bailiwick
I do not want to write a villanelle
I wish that I could somehow break their spell.

Heavy Lines

Light verse
weighs about
three words per ounce

Serious verse
on the other hand
gets about
seven words
to a pound

And Ezra Pound
will break the scales
at four words
to the ton.

Verse

Playing with rhyme takes time
There's near and false, sight and true
Internal, external, ten dollar, two for a dime
So much moon, June, balloon it makes you blue
It's easy to rhyme hope, mope, and dope
But translunar, sea schooner, and piano tuner
Take pushing and twisting a line to cope
With such almost and nearly and why didn't I sooner
Think of that. But hardest of all
(it's made me bald) is avoiding the nursery
Rhyme tune. It drives one up the wall
To hit rhyme after rhyme, in verse after versery
Line after line, a Mother Goose loose
Off her caboose, on the juice, short a deuce
Should hang by the noose, I have no more use
For such overdone, bad as a pun, too long in the sun
Stun like a gun, makes your bowels run, rhyme.

Dear Elizabeth

Mommy, as usual, was worried
and asked me to explain something.
She was afraid one day you would read
a play or poem I wrote
that said something not nice
about daughters, or babies, or being a daddy
and think I meant you
and think I didn't love you.

Mommy doesn't always understand about writing
how it takes parts of things
of events, of people, of feelings
and puts them together in new ways
that are part me, part not me,
some things added, and a lot left out.
Sometimes it's the love part that gets left out.

Sometimes it isn't about me, or you, at all.
There is one play Mommy thinks is about her
that talks about a daughter in a not-nice way
It was written even before you were conceived.

So, if you ever read anything I wrote
about little girls or babies or parents
and think it's not nice, remember
The love part got left out.

But in our lives, between me and you,
the love part
never gets left out.
I did, do, and will
love you
with every bit of love I've got.
Love,
Daddy.

Getting Dressed

My daughter believes
that getting dressed
on winter mornings
does not require
waking up.

Combing My Daughter's Hair

My daughter's hair
is long, blond, and tangled
Every morning
it's brush, brush, brush, brush
Until I gleam
        from the polish of its touch.

The Nude

The oil painting
over my desk
of the nude girl
is a memory
of my father

In his last days
amid the chemo
and radiation
he hung her
by his bedside
an unfather—
unpreacher—act

After his death
she came to me
and on my wall
looks down
with some
paternal secret
important, yes
meaningful, but
a secret
I cannot read
in the curves
and smile
he chose to view
as his life ebbed
and went away.

No Iambic

No iambic
pentameter
quatrain, sonnet
a b a b
c c d d
for me, oh no
I count sylla.

Pretending to Nap

I play with my daughter
by pretending to nap
while she piles dolls around me
and paints makeup on my face
it makes her happy
and lets me think
but she is disappointed
when I do not laugh
in surprise
when I wake
she wonders if I ever laugh
I say "Sometimes"
she says once a year
maybe
and she is right
I guess I am
a better father
asleep.

For Us All

The mountains do not cry
brooks do not sob
but I can sit
by the stream
and weep
for us all.

At Five

My daughter, at five
is afraid to go to sleep
for fear of monsters
stalking the night

I, at forty-five
crave the release of sleep
from the fear of monsters
stalking the day.

Divide

Standing on the Continental Divide
watching the future flow away
in one direction or another
wondering on which side
my drop of life will fall.

The Office

Sterile green cubicle
filled by babbling voices
and white noise
roofless, doorless, colorless
inhabited by personnel
who used to be people.

October 13, 1996

On October 13, 1996
my daughter
lost her first baby tooth
three days later
I became
Forty-six years
long in the tooth

Looking a horse
in the mouth
is rude
but informative

My daughter
danced with delight
at this evidence
of her maturing
my birthday was more somber
but
she is growing up
and
I am growing old.

Once Upon A Time

Once upon a time
a long, long time ago
maybe even a whole week ago
in a land far, far away
too far to walk to
in less than an hour
there lived a little girl
who was really a princess
but of course, nobody knew that
not even her parents
who only thought
she was real special
Anyway, this little girl
being six years old
knew everything
or at least thought she did
though she wasn't sure
what number came
after googooplus
or how to make a Z
without getting it backwards
but she could find
the Cartoon Network
by herself
and pour her own milk
if the carton wasn't too full
and get dressed by herself
if there weren't too many buttons
The only reason
she didn't do all the cooking herself
was that she wasn't allowed
to turn on the stove
and she thought she could drive a car

except she didn't have a license
This special little princess
had lots of sisters
who were all really dolls
so she lived alone
with her parents
who weren't much fun
always working or cooking or cleaning
  or writing plays or making crafts
  or applying for jobs or talking on the phone
She tried to invite friends over to play
but her mommy had to ask their mommy
and the mommies could never work things out
as easily as the kids could have
so lots of times she ended up alone
with her dolls and toys and TV
  and books and computer and keyboard
or she had to go with her parents
shopping or to parties or to restaurants
that didn't even give away balloons
So the little girl had to go to school
  and the after-school program
  and church on Sunday
  and dance class
  and art class
  and gymnastics
  and never had time
    to watch all thirty-six episodes
    of Scooby Doo
    or Garfield
    or the Flintstones
    and almost never got to see
      the Jetsons
    because it was on
      after eight at night

        and she had homework to do
        (though her parents did help
        because sometimes she had trouble
        even though she was very smart)
        and baths to take and teeth to brush and floss
        and it all took so much time
        and she was supposed to be asleep
        by nine o'clock on school nights
 So anyway, this tall, beautiful princess
thinking about all these things
decided to see if she could grow up
while no one was looking
and see if anybody would notice
so she did, but nobody paid any mind
So, after a while, she went back
to being a little girl
which, you must admit,
was the princess thing to do.

Scars

The scars mark off the years
like scratches on a prison wall
circumcision, tonsils, adenoids
muscle biopsies, acne
super-pubic catheter, prostate
excised illusions, reconfigured heart
in the end
we die
from too many scars.

Elizabeth's Pictures

In my office
pictures
form years
of little faces
getting wiser
all the time.

Kure Beach Terns

Stiff wind out of the north
Too cool for swimming
but fine for hovering
imitating the fishermen on the pier
we toss bits of bread aloft
and are suddenly swarmed
by what my daughter
thinks are seagulls
riding the wind
at arm's length
before our faces
"Toss it up!" I yell
as we stare at motionless wings
just beyond reach
black heads with white bodies
stacked on each layer of air
instantly shifting the few inches
to our errant throws
to gulp our offering
to their courage
to come so near
the dangerous tourists
visiting their sandy domain
it is a miracle of aerobatics
catching in waiting beak
a crust heaved skyward
quicker than I can blink
They surround us now
tens, dozens, scores
almost touching wings
in a formation no human fliers
would dare attempt
I have held hawks

uplifted on my arm
and had pigeons peck seeds
inches from my feet
but never before
have I stood
beside a bird in flight
hanging unmoving before me
no fear in its eyes
calmly treading air
until my bit of bread
found its place
in the flock
My daughter laughs
and I do too
tearing bread into bites
for hungry terns
who fill us with delight.

Every Time

Every time I think of you
Lying, a babe, in my arms
I get all squishy inside
Zestfully, I remember
All the days you grew
Before my eyes
Even now, far too big
To hold, you are what I
Hold in my heart.

Visiting

Visiting places I lived long ago
my father's home
my childhood beach
I expected them to change
to be less than my memory
smaller and shabbier than
my child's protected view
and they were
What was not expected
was that those left behind
still saw their homes
with children's eyes.

For My Daughter

For my daughter,
Life is getting less poetic
there are no odes to braces
dyslexia does not rhyme
with anything attractive
being nine in 1999
must be like 666
and other unfortunate numbers
occupational therapy
does not have the sound
of ballet classes
being cute is over
and it's hard to be pretty
after inheriting
your mother's tummy
and your poor parents
girding themselves to discuss sex
have no answers to why
kids become mass murderers
of kids
or why grownups
would shoot little Jewish kids
or their own kids
another innocence
is being lost
the warm blanket
that Mommy and Daddy
can take care of me
is unraveling too soon
to face third grade
in these days
requires a different courage
steeling her eyes
glistening in mine.

I Love You More

I love you more
than there are stars
she said to me
an eight-year-old's
attempt at poetry
worried I was growing old
at forty-eight
when do you plan to die?
she asked, as if a man
controlled that date
and then she pointed out to me
each item in her room
by which she could
remember me
ever the good daddy
I calmed her fears
and said I planned to be
around for years
until she was grown
and on her own at least
and eased her off to sleep
cuddling her blankie
between two large dolls
Lydia and Louise
but fathers lie
out of full hearts
and I have no more claim
on tomorrow than anyone
Elizabeth, I will try
to live forever
to kiss your child
or cheer your fate
but if I do not
know forever
my love will.

Dancing with My Daughter

Dancing with my daughter at her teacher's wedding
was complicated
beyond the fact that neither of us really knows how to dance
and were mostly just swaying to the music
while the wedding party jigged and jived barefoot on the church lawn
and beyond the lingering remnants of my Baptist anti-dance raising
by the effect of a ten-year-old in a thirteen-year-old's body
who has seen too many TV shows and has a bad Electra complex
trying to attach herself like I was her boyfriend instead of her father
catching me between wanting to hold my little girl
and having the proper fatherly attitude toward this new young woman
sprouting on fast forward toward adolescence
leaving me rushing to adjust to each new phase
that seems to come and go
before I realize that she has danced away from me again.

Holding

The first time I held my daughter
hours old and half an arm long
like most new fathers
I was afraid I would drop her
Three years later
just home from the hospital
still weak and feeble
I sat in a chair
and they placed her on my lap
toddler now, unsteady
on her own two feet
we were both a little scared
I would not be able to hold her
By seven she was too big to lift
and had to slide into my lap
by nine she was big as a small woman
and almost too heavy to hold
under any circumstances.
Now she sits beside me
and we hold each other
fearing the days coming
when I cannot hold her
and the further day
when she will have to hold me.

Time Doesn't Run

Time doesn't run
or flow
or stand still
it is consumed
into some event horizon
that bends our universe
to its will
making us a faint glow
around a black, lightless center.

Youth Elder

My church has a "Youth Elder"
some poor teen each year
selected to be made old
aged by responsibility
rotated from pillar to post
to learn how churches are run
and to speak for those still young
to those grown old
an admirable intent
if oxymoronic
but what we really need
is an "Elder Youth"
an old geezer
selected to be young again
for a year
allowed to run with the pack
to the pizza parties
to flirt and nuzzle
gulp soda and sing songs
and not have to think
about why churches are run.

My War

My daughter dances
to Sandman
by America
a '70s song
about draft dodgers
in a war
she knows nothing about
except a black slab
in Washington
and a story
about draft numbers
on T-shirts
I told her
to explain why
I was not in
my war.

Great-Grandparents

My mother sent me a picture
of my great-grandparents
and their children
taken about 1890
by a traveling photographer
the parents sit
on chairs moved outside
for the light
in their Sunday best
surrounded by eight children
almost grown
including my grandfather
with a little youth left in him
standing behind in the line
but his parents are old
ancient
my great-grandfather
has eyes that saw the Civil War
through gunpowder and smoke
in more battles
in Northern Virginia
than he cares to remember
but the most ancient
is the mother
like the nightmare of age
she sits in black
more worn than the soldier
staring at the camera
and through its lens
at me and mine
a glint of light
a slice of time
passed down to me
to see what was
and what may be.

051801

Sitting around a Denny's one night
with a bunch of Baptist virgins
of mixed high school age
back in the long ago days
when most high schoolers
actually were virgins
some brave soul asked
what does "horny" mean?
The Senior replied
it's the way guys
and I guess girls too
(oh yes, from the girl next to him)
get when they haven't had sex for awhile
which for most of us
was at least sixteen years
not counting the various solo arts
which left the impression
the Senior was not quite as horny
as the rest of us
but left us unsure
about the girl
but all amazed
we could be horny
and talk about it
at Denny's.

Drought

The lakes are low
the shoreline is yards from shore,
like dreams from reality
tree stumps that have not seen light
since the dam was born
poke up like old poems
scraping the bottom
of boats as ill-suited
for low water
as men for hard times
other boats are docked on mud
tied to ramps whose floats don't
moored tightly as jobs
The heat of summer is coming
but not rain
Undrinkable words abound,
but not what is needed
no dramatic thunder
or flashes of insight
only hot, dry air
and honestly burning sun.

052401

Driving my daughter to school
late already because of a lost CD
she has to have for dance class later
we see a rainbow
climbing into the dark day
bright enough to see the secondary
arching fainter alongside
and beyond the trees
the other end curving down
out of the black morning rain
lit by the rising sun behind us
two bright ends and a missing middle
sun behind, rain ahead, on we go
turning away to follow the road
a glimpse through the trees
and it is gone.

Toe Shoes

Satin-covered wood
padding and straps
pink slippers
to dream in
grace floating
in little girl nights
balanced on pain
and desire
because it is there
because it is hard
because somebody said
it is beautiful
pink clouds adrift
over hardwood earth
the young girls
go on toe.

On This Rock

Night rubs against the rough rock
like black acid
vapors rise unseen
scattering molecules
of what was
into the universe
to rejoin the ground of being
such is the rock nirvana
to be ground away
until there is no more there
there
the paradise
of not being
those who saw no reward
for those pebbles
that faded into dust
saw being there
as suffering
and those rocks
that have gone into the ground
tell no tales
of fiery underworlds
of volcanic rebirths
or cool streamsides
granite or limestone
they come and they go
like us
only slow.

Dust and Ashes

When the human body
is subject to intense heat
say, exploding aviation fuel
followed by burning walls and floors
that get hot enough to melt steel
in very tall buildings,
about all that's left
is dust and ashes
that are scattered
to the streets below
and blown over the harbor.
This leaves, for some souls,
no body to be found
nothing to identify
nothing to bury,
leaving those awaiting
those who have blown away
tasting tears
amid the dust and ashes.
So to mourn
we don sackcloth
and ashes
we breathe the dust
of those who were
we taste bitter ashes
on our tongues
And take within ourselves
forever
the dust and ashes.

Midnight thirty

Mommy, if I can't get to sleep by midnight thirty,
can I come to your room?
asked the little girl
who was good at many things
but not at going to sleep
Yes, dear, but you have to wait
till you see midnight thirty
on your clock on the shelf.
It's nine thirty now, so you have plenty of time
to dream dreams and plan plans
to sing songs in your mind
and imagine being all grown up
and if you're still awake
at midnight thirty
then you may come to our room
and wake up Daddy
and he will get a blanket and pillow
and lie down on the floor
in your room
so you can sleep.
And so, content that there was salvation
if the dark went on too long
the little girl
peacefully
went to sleep.

Traffic

Red and white rivers
crosscurrents flowing
in the dark evening
never touching, we hope
no churning into metal eddies
no waves crashing over us
just swift streams
lighting the way home.

Before My Eyes

Before my eyes
during the space
of some Nickelodeon music video
by some barely pubescent boy group
artificially manufactured by some producer
she changes
the metamorphosis begins
my hand on her shoulder
she suddenly giggles
"He's so cute," she says
of some Hollywood clone
selected by focus groups
and mall intercepts
as being the cute one
he may even sing on key
though the sound is so layered
and reengineered
it's impossible to tell
what his real voice would be like
but he's cute
I give him that
cute enough to move my daughter
from boy-hating
to adolescent crush
"He's probably a jerk," she continues,
"but he's sooooo cute."
An image of her teen years
flashes before me
boys and jerks
and how to tell
one from another
an essential skill
that must be learned

with at least a dash
of bitter experience
she giggles again
and blushes at her own
budding femininity
she will be OK, I think
so wise already
to know jerkdom
is possible
even in the terminally cute
she will grow painfully
wiser yet
but she will be OK
but my own pain
changes
with a shift
almost as profound
the little girl
daddy's little girl
is leaving
and the teen
is inward bound.

Stages

My wife gave me a list
of the stages of adolescence
purporting to describe
the psychological changes
the normal teenager
goes through
on the path to maturity
having missed most of these stages myself
I found it very instructive
the slow process
to independence
sexuality
and responsibility
that is necessary
for the girl
to become the woman
and the child
to become the adult
and the father
to become
the sad old man.

Fireflies

Green velvet dark
mating lights waltzing
love's fireworks
on shirtless nights

turn out the lights
if we can't see the stars
maybe this will do
Tinkerbell in the woods

and we are lost boys
chasing fairy dust
that sparkles
among the leaves

minuscule lightning
but no jar tonight
precious glory flies free
lighting memory

Daughter, can you ever know
how precious miracles are
lovelights of home
flit on the darkening sky.

Calling Schools

Calling schools to ask
who wants to teach
my daughter
for the next six years
reveals a problem
they seem to think
I should be grateful
they would even consider
admitting her
and I am convinced
they are the ones
receiving the privilege.

Dyslexia

When the kaleidoscope spins
throwing light around like balls
in a kid's fun factory
it's hard to see the star
in the dark beyond the light
to see the future lit by the past
a far-off blaze that will only show up
after the evening sun has set
and we turn our eyes to the night
but sometimes
beyond the prisms and mirrors
there is a hint of what will come
further along
"Elizabeth reads well," the teacher said
and the galactic glow pierced the day
promising starlight
hinting at a star
beyond the light of day.

Dark Clouds

Dark clouds
wind
remnants of tornados
that killed in Kansas City
now blowing over Atlanta
scaring the birds and wives
bragging of destruction
houses splintered
cars transported
mobile homes never to be found
and bodies lying quietly
under bathtubs
bare of walls
waiting to be found.

In Less than a Month

In less than a month
she will be thirteen
officially a teen
neigh six feet tall
bigger and stronger
than her old man
still not sure about seventh grade
middle school, middle youth
moving into volleyball and basketball
holding on still to dance
transitions and changes
holding on and letting go
no more children's prices
now she eats and sleeps grownup
PG-13 the movies say
and I try to remember
that it is the PG
that still counts.

Beach

On the white sand
crowded with bikinis
and an occasional thong
she sat back from the waves
on a large towel
shaded by a big umbrella
covered with a Moslem scarf
high-neck shirt
and long pants
modesty intact
among the bare infidels
as she breastfed
her new baby.

Writing Out the Junk

Writing out the junk
Digging for bedrock
By tossing out the first
Then second
Then third idea
Going for oil
Or diamonds
Down deep
Where the rocks are hot
And the pressure steep
Where the digging takes drills
And men sweat
And die.

Watching My Daughter

Watching my daughter play basketball
it occurs to me
how much difference
confidence makes
she seems to have
my fatal flaw
of thinking too much
about what she does not know
the hesitation
to evaluate all the possibilities
to look for the safe choice
staying within the confines
of her coaching
and never
just driving to the basket.

In the End

In the end
it is not life or time or wisdom
that is lost
it is memories
no one else will ever know
that disappear
crying alone on the street corner
the spring break I first kissed a nipple
listening to my father haggle over bongos in Mexico
taking supper to my father when he worked in the jail
seeing my mother literally kneeling in prayer one early morning
rocking my daughter to sleep singing a Paul Simon song
gone are the days
and no one else will know
to mourn their passing.

The Rain Is Creeping In

The rain is creeping in
cloud shadows sweep across the ground
my daughter once asked
Daddy, did you ever chase a cloud?
No, I said, but I did used to watch
    the cloud shadows fly across the brown mountains
    in the deserts of Arizona
even wrote a long-forgotten poem about it
    though I did not tell her that part
But chase a cloud? Don't they go too fast
    or fade away and reform
    or merge so you can't tell one from another?
To run after an edge of light
    passing through a moment of life
    lost way up in the sky
How childish
Like writing a poem
or dreaming in the day.

Passage—First Driving Lesson

On the Fourth of July
expressing his independence
the basketball player
we watched in the boys' varsity games
after the girls played
choosing to be free of restraint
died unbuckled

On Saturday the eighth
in an empty lot
behind a medical building
across from the hospital
I handed my fifteen-year-old
clutching her still-warm permit
the keys to the car
for the first time
as soon as she was strapped in
praying to the god of seatbelts
airbags, and adolescents
and spent the first lesson
teaching how to brake.

An Old Picture

It's an old picture, black and white
1920-something, bright sunny day
my mother the girl
three sisters and little brother
(where were the three older sisters?)
smiling at having their picture taken
an event back then
especially for mountain kids
so poor they wouldn't notice
when the Depression came
Here they are, still young
elementary school age it looks
happy, grinning, outside in play clothes
eyes alight in sunshine, summer
not seeing past that day
no shadows in this photograph
no image of the car crash
that will kill the youngest girl
bright eyes looking directly at the camera
or the mysterious tropical disease
that will carry away the only son
while in the army just after WWII
despite the Tom Sawyer smile and overalls
Even those who shine in my memory
have eyes not yet darkened
by cancer or war or ill children or dead husbands
My mother lives on
She will be eighty-nine this summer
changed so that this girl
in the picture
needs a name on the back
to be recognized
but it is her

eighty or so years ago
bright and sunny
the way I never knew her
her sun still on the rise.

Shuttle Landing

The bird from space
flew over the swamp
touching down on the incongruous concrete
sending the ibis and egrets flying away
only the eagle remained
circling the strange bird
riding the thermals and vented gasses
examining the rare creature
that flew higher than he.

Barcelona

Walking back from La Rambla
as my age began to show
my daughter took my arm
in the Spanish style
and began
to take care of me.

Graduation, Class of 2013

Despite the forecast
The sky had only puffy white shade
All morning
While the speeches were made
And the seven hundred graduates walked across the stage
Only after the luncheon
As the cars were packed
And the seniors drove off
One by one
Into wherever
Did the sky
Gently, quietly
Begin to weep.

Squirrel

The squirrel pauses
atop the stump of the old oak tree
remembering.

Aunt Dot

At my last aunt's funeral
(ninety-seven, WWII vet, five great-great-grandchildren)
as the procession drove to the cemetery
the on-coming cars, in the old way of small southern towns,
to show respect
pulled to the side of the road and stopped
to let the dead pass by
this made my wife cry.

December 2021

The inflatable Christmas decorations
(Frostys, Santas, elves, and reindeer)
lie prostrate across the lawn
powerless to rise
like survivors of a drunken orgy
on Sunday morning
Capturing, perhaps better than their upright selves
the deflated spirit
of a covid Christmas.

Sunset

Geese flying into the sunset
Say my own sun is setting
I do not fear being dead
I do fear dying
If there is a God anywhere close to good
He owes me one
If not, I do not fear being nothing
But from is to was sounds painful
Change never comes easy
So I do not fear the night
I fear the fading of the light.

About the Author

David Davis wrote a science fiction novel entitled *The Mistakes*, published by Kohler Books in 2020. In 2023, he also published a collection of essays on science and religion, *Seven Heretical Sermons*, and a collection of detective short stories, *The Detectives*. In addition, he has had seventeen plays produced, including productions in New York and Hollywood. He has also had several poems, magazine features, and scholarly articles published. He earned a PhD in Theatre and is a member of the Dramatists Guild and Working Title Playwrights. He has worked as a physics and math teacher, actor, head of three college theatre programs, technical writer, editor, and health communications specialist. He currently lives in Atlanta, Georgia, with his wife, Kathy, and has one daughter, Elizabeth.

Other Books by David Davis

Compiled Poems: 1957-2022

The Mistakes

Seven Heretical Sermons

The Detectives

Selected Plays of David Davis

www.ingramcontent.com/pod-product-compliance
Lightning Source LLC
Chambersburg PA
CBHW082200070526
44585CB00020B/2220